AN ILLUSTRAT
HISTORY OF
1066

Why Edward, Harold, Edgar and William were all kings of England that year

1066:

4 KINGS
3 BATTLES
2 INVASIONS
1 THRONE...

You will find the words highlighted in red in the GLOSSARY on page 43, which explains what these words mean.

Book design by Amanda Pollard

First published in Great Britain 2009 by WritersPrintShop
ISBN 1904623220

Acknowledgments

We would like to thank those who have helped make this book:

First, Will Jones for suggesting the team of writer and designer, and second Dave Pike for all his technical and practical support; Rachel Claye, who edited and combed through the ideas to make them more intelligible; and Verna Campbell for her input.

Thanks also to Alison Stewart of Bletchingdon Primary School for advising on the choice of words to ensure that young readers would be able to enjoy this adventure into our history.

All the (abundant) input and support from friends and family is much appreciated.

And finally gratitude and respect is due to the ancient scribes and historians who have left us so much information and enough puzzles to keep us guessing.

SOME KINGS OF ENGLAND

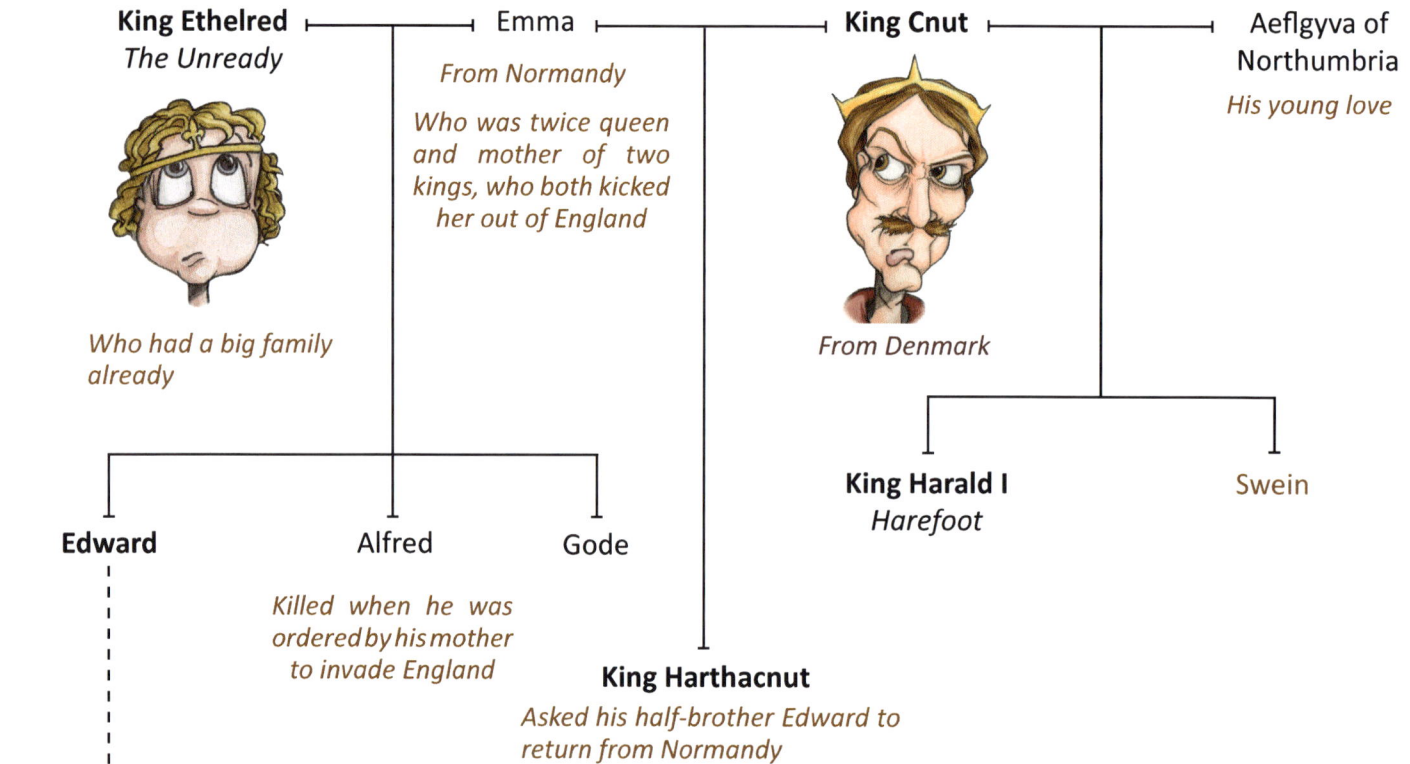

King Ethelred
The Unready

Emma

From Normandy

Who was twice queen and mother of two kings, who both kicked her out of England

King Cnut

Aeflgyva of Northumbria

His young love

Who had a big family already

From Denmark

King Harald I
Harefoot

Swein

Edward

Alfred

Gode

Killed when he was ordered by his mother to invade England

King Harthacnut

Asked his half-brother Edward to return from Normandy

So when Harthacnut died young (and suddenly - just like Cnut and Harold!) Edward became king in 1042

*He is known as **Edward the Confessor***

He married Harold Godwinson's sister, Edith. They had no children but 'adopted' Edgar, Margaret and Christina, whose grandfather was Edward's half-brother.

*Their great-great-great-great-grandfather was King Alfred (who we also know as **Alfred The Great**)*

THE GODWINSON FAMILY

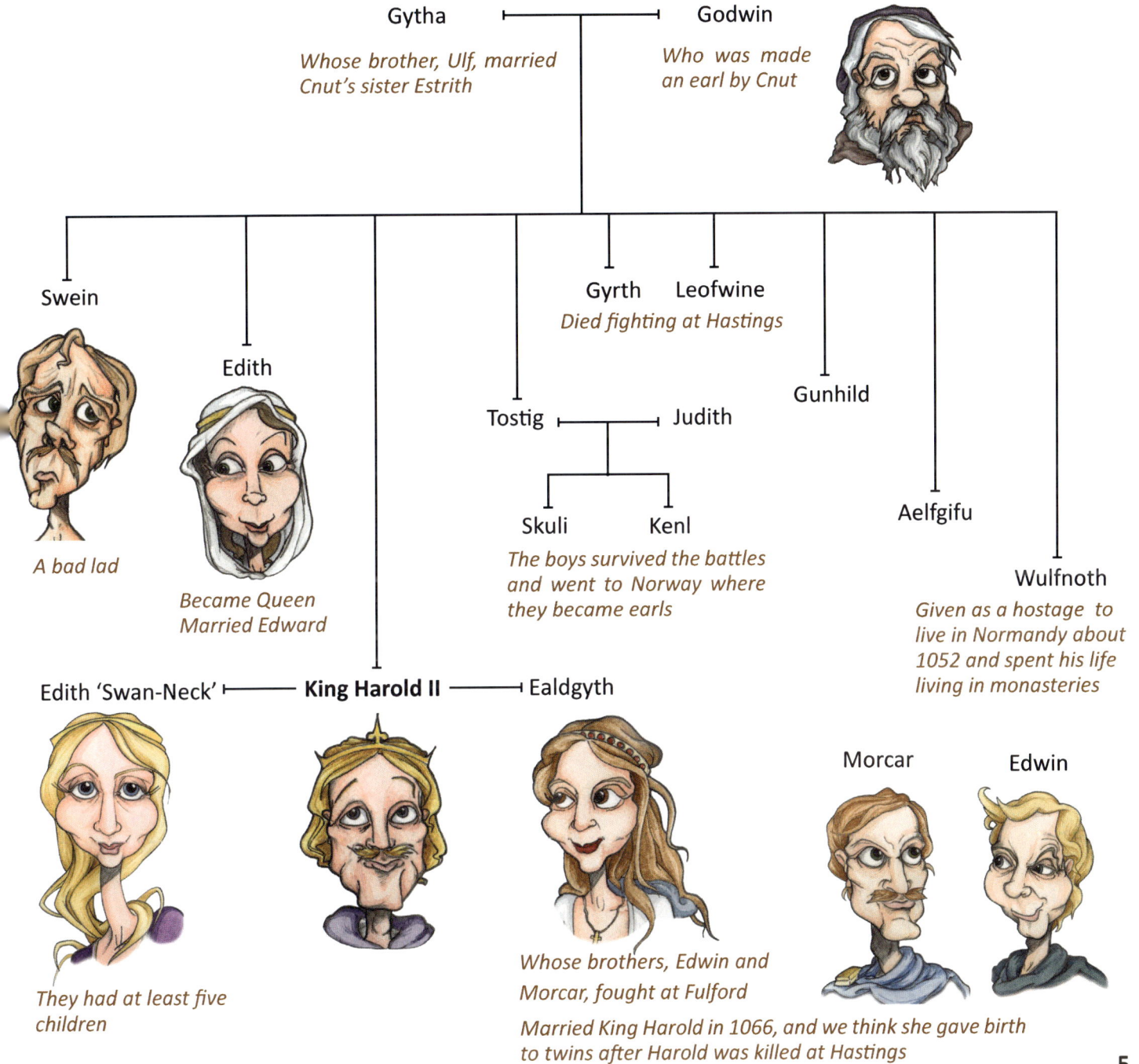

Gytha

Whose brother, Ulf, married Cnut's sister Estrith

Godwin

Who was made an earl by Cnut

Swein

A bad lad

Edith

Became Queen Married Edward

Gyrth   Leofwine

Died fighting at Hastings

Tostig ┤ ├ **Judith**

Gunhild

Skuli   Kenl

The boys survived the battles and went to Norway where they became earls

Aelfgifu

Wulfnoth

Given as a hostage to live in Normandy about 1052 and spent his life living in monasteries

Edith 'Swan-Neck' ┤ ├ **King Harold II** ─── ┤ **Ealdgyth**

They had at least five children

Morcar   Edwin

Whose brothers, Edwin and Morcar, fought at Fulford

Married King Harold in 1066, and we think she gave birth to twins after Harold was killed at Hastings

5

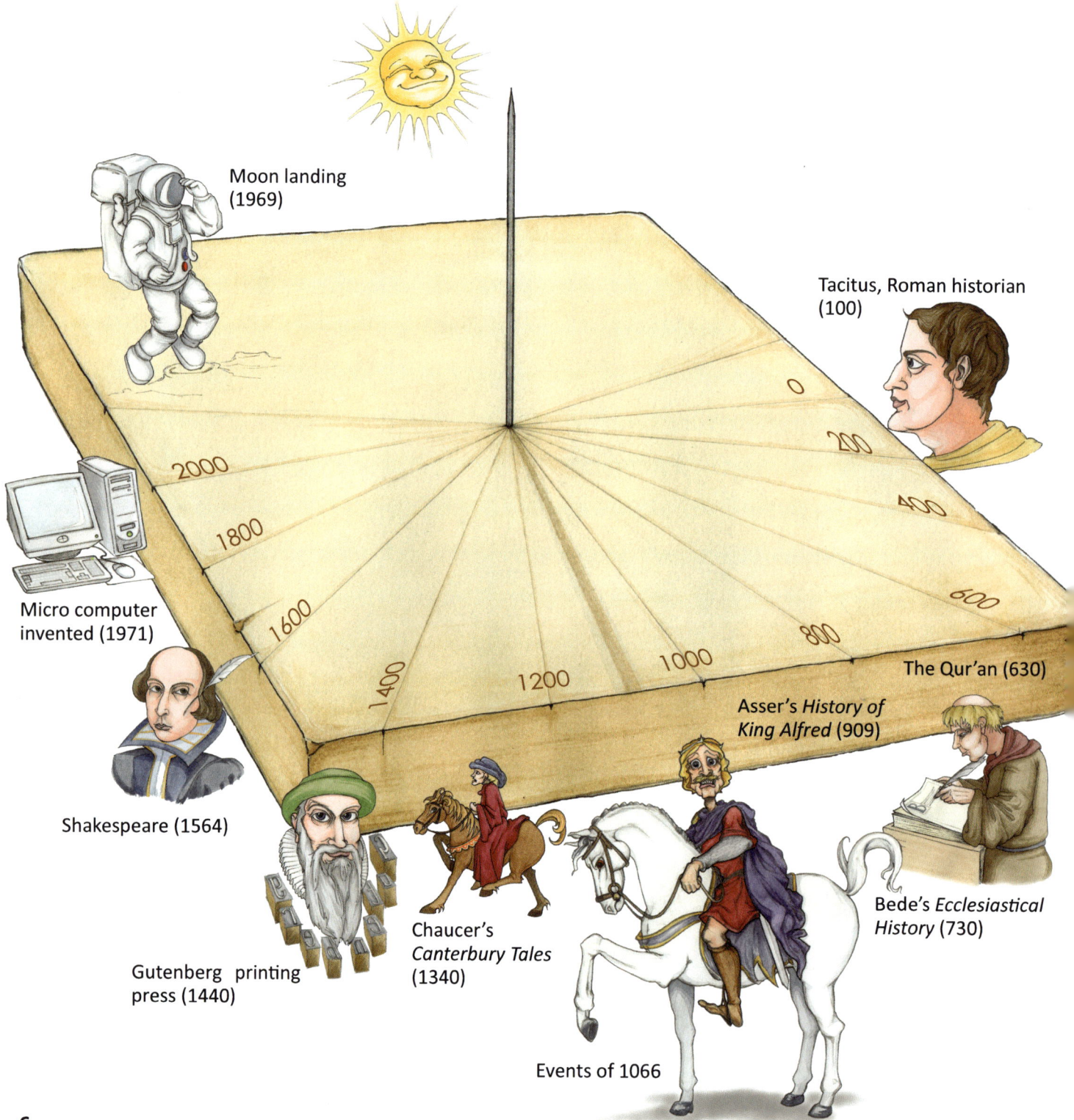

Moon landing (1969)

Tacitus, Roman historian (100)

Micro computer invented (1971)

2000

1800

1600

1400

1200

1000

800

600

400

200

0

Shakespeare (1564)

The Qur'an (630)

Asser's *History of King Alfred* (909)

Gutenberg printing press (1440)

Chaucer's *Canterbury Tales* (1340)

Events of 1066

Bede's *Ecclesiastical History* (730)

DURING 1066, ENGLAND HAD FOUR KINGS. THIS IS THE EXCITING STORY OF THAT YEAR...

The old king Edward died just as the new year began. King Edward was very religious and history remembers him as Edward the Confessor because he spent so much time praying. Edward had ordered that a stone church be built and he lived just long enough to see it completed. The new abbey was called the West Minster because it was built to the west of the old Roman city of London.

In those days, all the most powerful people would gather at the king's court for the traditional festivals we call Christmas and Easter. Although the king was in charge, they would discuss issues of the day and give the king their advice and support. This was such a good idea that almost 1000 years later, people still meet and govern the country from the old king's palace. We know it as Parliament but it is really the Palace of Westminster.

The leaders were all there for Edward's funeral on January 6th and selected Harold as the new king. Harold's coronation had to be rushed as January 6th was the last day of the Christmas festival and many of the important people were ready to start their journey home. Kings and queens of England are still crowned in Edward's church, which we now call Westminster Abbey.

Queen Elizabeth II's coronation, 1953

How do we know this?
Monks kept a record of the events from each year. We call these various diaries the Anglo-Saxon Chronicle. It is interesting to see what some scribes included and others ignored. The monks and nuns who did the writing tell us a lot about church matters. So we know about the building and consecration of the abbey, but the chronicle tells us very little about ordinary life.

7

To understand the importance of what happened in 1066 we need to go back further in time - to when Edward's father, King Ethelred, came to the throne as a young boy, perhaps 10 years old. His mother was said to have organised the murder of his half-brother at Corfe Castle so her son could become king. She then appointed some people to help her run the country for him.

England was regarded as a peaceful and prosperous country. But then a series of coastal raids began. The raiders were Vikings - people who came from the Norse lands we now think of as Norway and its neighbours. King Ethelred was still young and there were no strong army leaders to organise the English defence.

So the raiders were paid to go away with a lot of silver, called Danegeld. This was not a good plan. Even more Vikings came back and were given more silver. Soon the Vikings came and stayed. This time they were given money not to fight. So King Ethelred got the nickname 'Unred', which meant 'bad advice'. But we know him as Ethelred the Unready.

How do we know this?
The Chronicle tells us about a new wave of Viking raids in 980. The monks are careful to record all the damage done to churches, as well as the amount of money that was paid. We also have records of sermons given by bishops claiming that the Vikings were being sent as a punishment. They said people should behave better and pray more. One bishop said the fashion for long hair was one cause of England's troubles!

8

King Ethelred was descended from King Alfred the Great. Alfred had stopped the Vikings from taking over the whole of England 200 years earlier. The word 'king' just means somebody is from the right family, like the word 'kin'. Belonging to the right family was important if you wanted to be king.

In 1066, the new King Harold was not from Alfred's kin. But his sister, Edith, had been married to King Edward who was. They had no children, but she was looking after Alfred's only surviving family, Ethelred's great-grandchildren Edgar and Margaret. Edgar was only a boy and not ready to lead an army. This may be why the powerful people meeting that Christmas chose Harold to be their king instead.

England needed a strong king because other rulers wanted its rich land. At this time the borders of countries were not fixed and attacking weaker neighbours was common.

And we know this because...
Queen Edith arranged for a book to be written about her husband, King Edward, and the book tells us a lot about her own family. She tells us how she looked after young Edgar and his sister Margaret. (Margaret later married the king of Scotland, where she introduced the English language and English church practices to Scotland and is remembered as St Margaret.)

9

Earl Godwin was Harold and Edith's father. Godwin had served four kings and was married to a Danish wife, Gytha, so King Harold was half Danish. The old king had been a peaceful man and did not have an army of his own. Instead he relied on Earl Godwin and the other English earls to defend England.

At one point King Edward was threatened by the king of Norway, who claimed that he should be king of England instead. Edward replied that he would not fight and they would have to come and kill him as he sat on his throne. No one did.

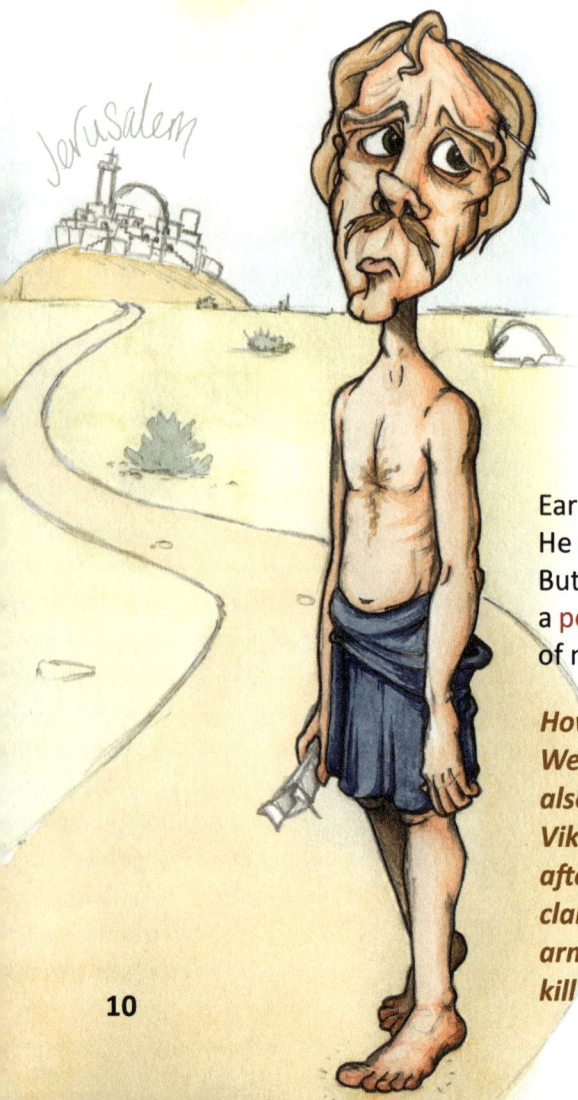

Earl Godwin and Gytha had a large family. The eldest son, Swein, was very bad. He abducted a nun on one occasion and later killed one of his Danish cousins. But eventually he repented and walked to Jerusalem without his boots on as a penance. Somewhere on the way back he died leaving Harold, who was one of nine children, as the oldest living son.

How do we know this?
We know about the English events from the Anglo-Saxon Chronicle, but we also have a fuller story from various sagas of the Norse lands, where the Vikings came from. The saga of the Kings of Norway tells us that in 1043, just after Edward became king, King Magnus of Norway sent letters to Edward claiming he should be king of England. Edward said that he didn't have an army so he would sit on the throne and they would just have to come and kill him. They didn't.

Families can be very complicated.

King Ethelred's second wife, Queen Emma, had been born in Normandy, in France. So when the Danish King Cnut conquered England the royal couple fled to her family in Normandy with their three children. But after King Ethelred died, Emma went back to England to marry King Cnut. While Emma became queen again, poor Edward was stranded in Normandy and studied religion because he did not ever expect to be king, as Cnut and Emma had more children.

As a young man Cnut had attacked England with his father, and fallen in love with Aelfgyva of Northampton. They had at least two sons before Cnut had to leave England. In time King Cnut became king of Denmark, England and Norway.

But when Cnut died suddenly, both Emma and Aelfgyva wanted their sons to be king. Aelfgyva's son Harold Harefoot was made king first. He also died suddenly and Emma's son, Harthacnut, who was already king in Denmark, became king of England. But he died two years later.

So Edward returned from Normandy and became king in 1042. He did not trust his mother, and one of his first acts as king was to take away all her treasure and force her to leave England.

How do we know this?
The Chronicle of the Kings of Norway was written down about 150 years after these events by Snorri Sturluson. Snorri was one of the chief judges in Iceland and recognised the importance of recording things. In the introduction to his saga he says that he will only allow to be written down those things he has received from reliable sources. This is what all historians try to do. The Anglo-Saxon Chronicle explains how England managed to avoid a civil war when there were so many possible kings at the time of King Cnut's death .

England had at least four strong armies, but their leaders were not very experienced as there had not been any big battles in England for a long time. Early in 1066 it was discovered that the king of Norway planned to attack England. His name was also King Harald, though he had a nickname, 'Hardrada', which means 'Ruthless Ruler' in old Norse. In Normandy, Duke William was demanding that he should be king as he said that Edward had promised the land to him.

To make matters worse, King Harold's younger brother Tostig was helping those who wanted to invade England. Tostig was probably angry because he had been forced to leave England late in 1065 to live with his wife's family in Flanders. The people around York had not liked the way he taxed them and imposed new laws, so they did not want him as their earl.

Harold was King Edward's chief minister at the time his brother was forced out. The English chronicle says the king wanted Harold to help Tostig, but Harold preferred to compromise and keep the peace. He may even have thought Tostig was in the wrong: the northern earls who had forced him out, two brothers called Edwin and Morcar, were angry because their father had been sent into exile so Tostig could become an earl.

How do we know this?
The English chroniclers record the bare facts of the revolt against Tostig and Harold's peace-making. It looks as if the northern earls, Edwin and Morcar, were prepared to fight King Edward and Earl Harold (before he was king) to keep Tostig out. One French chronicle suggests that Tostig was plotting with Duke William and King Harald of Norway. The Norwegian sagas agree with this view.

King Harold had to make a difficult political decision when he became king. Edwin and Morcar were important earls in the north. Harold needed to have them on his side if he wanted to keep the country united, even though they had forced his brother out. Tostig was furious that Harold would not let him come back and he decided to cause trouble. Unfortunately, we are not sure what Tostig planned. His sister Edith said Tostig was too clever for his own good but never told people about his plans.

We think Tostig sent messengers to Duke William and probably offered advice on the best way to conquer England. Tostig knew the strengths and possible weaknesses of England and had fought alongside his brother several times, so could guess what Harold might do.

Tostig's cousin Sweyn was King of Denmark. Tostig travelled north and tried to persuade King Sweyn to help restore him to his position in England. But King Sweyn offered Tostig land in Denmark instead. He even offered to make Tostig an earl in Denmark because he did not want a war with his cousin Harold. Tostig was rude to Sweyn and sailed north to try and persuade King Harald of Norway to attack England.

How do we know this?
The Norse sources tell us a great deal about the meetings in Denmark and Norway. But because Tostig left no record we are guessing, which often happens with history. Queen Edith's book is quite sympathetic to Tostig and we get the impression he was her favourite brother, so she does not tell any tales.

13

King Harald of Norway eventually agreed to invade England. He sent a summons for an army to assemble from all around his land. In those days Norway included much of what is now Sweden.

When the Norsemen were ready to sail, King Harald made his son Magnus, who was about 18, the new king of Norway. Harald then took his wife, his two daughters and his youngest son Olaf with him in his longship.

King Harald was a tall man of about 50, and the most feared warrior of his age. He was very cunning. When besieging one town he pretended to be dead and his men asked permission to bury him at a church in the town. When the long coffin - which actually contained weapons rather than a body - was at the gate, they turned it sideways to hold the gates open long enough for his men to rush in and capture the place.

How do we know this?
We have to be cautious about old stories unless there is other evidence. But the story about the coffin comes from a reliable source and is typical of Harald's character, so it is probably true. Not all ancient writings are designed to be read as history. Some writers liked to make the story more exciting. There are times when we have to judge if the writer is a historian or a storyteller. Shakespeare was a storyteller who wanted his plays to be exciting. He had to be careful not to upset the rich and powerful, so we do not call him a historian just because he wrote about history.

HARALD R.I.P. (unless joking...)

14

King Harald brought only half his army and left the rest at home for his son Magnus. His fleet of about 300 longships would take about a week to reach England. King Harald stopped in the Orkney Isles to leave his family in a safe place until he had conquered England.

The fleet then sailed to Scotland where Tostig was waiting. Earlier in the summer, Tostig had taken many English ships from their base at Sandwich. He then used the ships to raid the English coast but was careful to avoid a battle. Eventually most of his ships left him and went back to England, and the small army he had brought from Flanders returned home.

How do we know this?
We are still relying on the Norse sagas, but the English chronicle tells us about Tostig's raids. We always need to be careful when we find numbers quoted because we think old stories have a tendency to exaggerate. But the number of ships fits with the size of fleet that could have been assembled based on what happened before and after.

When the Norse army reached England it attacked Scarborough. This allowed the warriors to get off their ships and stretch their legs after crossing the North Sea. It was also an opportunity for Tostig to take revenge against the rebels who had thrown him out. As it was harvest time there was plenty of food available, so the army marched south, raiding as it went.

Perhaps the clever King Harald hoped the raids would lure the English army to rush to defend the coast and leave York undefended.

Keeping the land and its people safe was the most important duty of an Anglo-Saxon leader. If leaders failed in their duty to protect the peace they would soon be replaced. But Earl Morcar did not try to chase the invaders, which is just as well because if he had done he might have been caught out by King Harald's crafty plan.

How do we know this?
The attack on Scarborough is in the chronicles. Military leaders tend to be careful not to let people know their plans. They like to keep these secret so we are often forced to speculate about their motives and guess what they were planning.

16

The Norsemen were very good sailors. They knew that twice each year there are very high tides. The shape and direction of the mouth of the river Humber, which leads towards the city of York, creates a rather special condition: a small wave of water flows up the river. One moment the river is flowing towards the sea, and a few moments later it is going the other way. This is called a river bore, which comes from the Norse word *bara*.

So, during these high tides, instead of flowing for six hours one way and then six hours in the opposite direction, the river flows very fast for four hours and then ebbs for eight.

The River Humber, showing sandbanks near Riccall

The Norse seamen picked exactly the right days when the river's waters would rush them deep inland along the mighty River Humber which joins the River Ouse and flows through York. The flow carried them along much faster than anybody could row. The army stopped close (but not too close) to York at a place called Riccall, which became its base.

How do we know this?

We know people have been calculating the tides for centuries so it is possible to work out the time and the height of the tide in 1066. We know the date of the battle because it is recorded in the Anglo-Saxon Chronicle, although we have to do two more calculations. The date is related to a saint's day so we have to look at a religious calendar. But we also have to remember that we 'lost' some days because the Romans got the calculations of leap years just very slightly wrong.

There were two English armies waiting near York. Earl Edwin had brought his men from Mercia to Tadcaster and Earl Morcar had assembled his army of Northumbrians in York. The new King Harold had married their sister Ealdgyth in York Minster during the Easter festivities of 1066, and she was expecting twins. So the families were now united.

King Harold already had a lover who we know as Edith Swan-Neck. She was said to be a great beauty. They had three sons and two daughters who were already teenagers. Edith Swan-Neck seems to have accepted Harold's political marriage. Some chroniclers say she went to find Harold after the battle of Hastings.

How do we know this?
The English chronicles tell us a lot about the two earls, Edwin and Morcar. There are also several records telling of Harold's marriage in York. But we know little of Edith Swan-Neck. Much of what we think of as history is about the powerful, and until recently historians did not bother to tell us much about anybody else.

Edwin and Morcar were about 20 years old and had been brought up by their granny, Lady Godiva. She was famous for trying to stop her people being forced to pay too much tax. According to a story told in later years, she rode naked through the streets of Coventry and everyone agreed not to go out to the market that day so they would not embarrass her.

Edwin had become earl during Edward's reign when his father Aelfgar died. He was too young to stop his neighbour Earl Tostig from bringing his new cavalry across Mercia to attack Wales, Mercia's ally. Tostig's expedition was not successful but it was a good test for the new English cavalry. The Welsh leader, Prince Gryffud, was later betrayed and his head sent to King Edward.

In the tangled politics of this time, it was Gryffud's widow, Ealdgyth, that King Harold married in York to cement the alliance with Edwin and Morcar. So the twins that Queen Ealdgyth was expecting would have close family ties to both the leading earls helping to unite England. Women were sometimes referred to as 'peace-weavers' because their marriage and children helped bring rival families together.

How do we know this?
We know about the earls from the chronicles, but the story of Lady Godiva was written down much later and we will probably never know exactly what happened. But Godiva, or Godgifu, was a real figure and landowner who might well have done something spectacular for the benefit of her tenants. The early English historians, who all worked for the church, just did not record events such as this. It was left to later storytellers and we cannot rely on them as much as we do on historians.

19

The scene was set for a battle to defend the north.

King Harald of Norway started early. He led his army quickly towards York. He did not want to give the two big English armies time to join up. Harald had about 6,000 warriors which was not enough to defeat the two English armies together as they probably numbered 10,000.

The Mercian army could not cross the River Ouse without marching for most of a day. So Edwin was only able to bring a small force to help his brother Morcar. The rest of the army stayed at Tadcaster in case the Norse army decided to sail up the River Warfe and attack Mercia.

Earl Morcar assembled his army along the bank of a deep natural ditch that was about 40m wide. He had a very strong position. On the left he had the River Ouse and to the right he had some marshy land, and about 5,000 soldiers to fill the gap between these natural obstacles. The edges of the shield-wall are called the flanks. It is very, very important not to let an enemy get round the edges of the shield-wall to attack from the side or from behind.

Surprisingly, nobody recorded the size of armies at this time so we have to do a lot of calculating and estimating.

Earl Morcar's army of Northumbrians fought well and pushed the Norsemen back - but it was a trap. King Harald of Norway had told the weakest soldiers to attack first. That tempted the English army to come off the high ground on the bank of the ditch in order to force the attackers to retreat.

The trick worked. Earl Morcar was probably facing Earl Tostig, his bitter enemy and the man he had replaced as earl of Northumbria the year before. Perhaps his army knew this and expected him to go after Tostig even though it would have made more military sense to stay on the high ground - it is harder to attack uphill.

As Morcar's men came down the steep bank of the ditch to push the Norse army back, the Northumbrian line was stretched and became thinner as the middle bulged where Morcar was advancing. Because Morcar was now on lower ground, he was not able to see what was happening at the two flanks. So what happened next took him by surprise.

How do we know this?
Two Norse sagas describe the battle in detail. When compared with the landscape that existed in 1066, the sequence of events makes a great deal of sense. We have to use judgement and some informed guess-work to work out what happened if we only rely on the ancient descriptions, so it is very useful to include information from archaeology and geology.

King Harald now ordered his army to charge with a blast on a war-horn. Most of the Norse warriors crossed the ditch to do battle with the English shieldwall. But there is a little hill on the Norse side of the ditch near the river, where part of King Harald's army was hidden so Earl Edwin would not have guessed what was about to happen.

King Harald led a charge with his best men and managed to cross the ditch at the place where Earl Edwin was guarding the vital flank. King Harald was tall and strong. He said, *'I do not need a shield. My swinging axe is my shield'*. He could afford to be bold because he was supported by other good warriors armed with spears, swords, axes and shields who were ready to protect their leader.

After a short battle beside the river, the charge by King Harald's men forced Edwin back so that the Norsemen could cross the ditch. Morcar was too busy in the centre so he did not spot the danger until it was too late.

Soon the Norsemen were able to surround the Northumbrian army. Many of the English were trapped in the mud at the place which was later called Fulford. Fulford means something like 'muddy river crossing place'. So King Harald, with some help from the traitor Tostig, won the battle, although both Edwin and Morcar survived.

And how do we know this?
It is always nice to have several sources of information but we have two sagas with detailed and similar descriptions of the battle. The losers did not bother to keep a record apart from saying that the Norsemen 'possessed the field'. Historians writing in the next 100 years described a fierce battle and the English 'fleeing'. But all the sources have to be translated and sometimes words like 'ditch' or 'swamp' can be interpreted in a number of ways.

When the battle was over, the people of York probably closed the gates and feared the worst. But King Harald told them that if they joined him to help conquer England the following spring, he would not attack the city. The people of York held a meeting, called a Thing, where they decided that this was their only option. So they agreed to exchange hostages a few days later.

Hostages were normally men, and it was common for both sides to give the same number. Hostages would live just like members of the family and were well looked after. This was an established way to keep the peace in medieval society.

The Norsemen made their way back to Riccall, where there was doubtless some celebrating. We assume there were wounds to dress and weapons to repair, as well as the dead to bury, but the writers are silent about these practical matters.

How do we know about hostages?
English chroniclers often tell us about the exchange of hostages. They were not hostages in the modern sense. They were much more like ambassadors, although very occasionally hostages were held by an invader and there are a few examples of hostages being harmed when an agreement was broken.

Meanwhile, down south...

...England's King Harold had been waiting for the expected invasion from Normandy. But there was no sign of William - he apparently said the wind was not quite right. It was late in the year so Harold told his army to go home. His men had already been waiting for the Normans to arrive for over two months. The English had a small regular army and another force that was called the **Fyrd** (pronounced 'feared') and this expeditionary force was summoned when required.

Was sending the army home a trick? At any rate, the moment the army had disbanded Duke William set sail from Normandy. Duke William had been ready to sail for about six weeks. Was the delay a part of Tostig's plan, because he knew England was strong enough to defeat any one of the invaders but would be stretched to defend against two? Was it really likely there was no south-westerly wind for William's crossing? Or was William waiting, knowing there would be an invasion in the north? Then again, was William's fleet forced to stay in port because a strong English navy was patrolling the coast?

History leaves us many such questions to which we will never be certain of the answer.

What do we know?
Not enough! The chroniclers certainly tell us that Harold sent his army home. But this was written after the Norman invasion and probably after many of the monasteries had been filled with Norman abbots and monks. Under the system that was set up by King Alfred the Great, when one part of the Fyrd was released another could be assembled. So we are not sure if the chroniclers, who were not warriors, understood the whole story and they do not give us many details. Some of the Norman writers at the time do not support the story about the lack of wind and tell us it was wet and windy that harvest time.

24

Duke William's army did set out, but instead of sailing to England - as everyone expected - it landed further up the French coast. If William had sailed across to England at that time then he would have arrived just as King Harald of Norway was invading in the north. Is that what Tostig planned?

England's King Harold must have guessed this was a possibility, which is why he kept his army in the south. By occupying the Isle of Wight, the English were in a good position to ride in their longships and attack the Duke William's army wherever it landed.

Was William playing a clever game, trying to ensure the English army he would face was exhausted by battle in the north and lots of marching? Was it really part of William's plan to set sail and then head back to the French coast? The English chronicles report that the English fleet ran into a storm while returning to its base at Sandwich, so it is probable that the same storm hit the Norman fleet.

Why doesn't history always give us the whole story?
It is often said that the winner gets to write the history. As Harold eventually lost, we do not know if the withdrawal was a trick. By contrast, everything William did is related as if it was part of some master plan. The best evidence, written by a bishop, is that William intended to sail straight to England.

25

When Harold heard that William had not crossed the channel and was still in France, he returned to London. The news of the Norse landing in the north must have reached Harold almost as soon as he arrived at his base in Waltham Abbey. He immediately gathered an army to march north.

Harold took his new cavalry. The cavalry could move quickly but it would still take four days for an army to reach Tadcaster where the Mercian army was waiting. Harold was well travelled and had visited the lands we now call Germany, France and Italy. He would have learned on these journeys about the new way of fighting from horseback.

On his way north, the bad news would have reached him about the defeat of the Northumbrians at Fulford. Harold had to do some quick thinking.

How do we know this?
We learn about the use of cavalry from the Anglo-Saxon Chronicle. While Harold was still an earl, he and his brother Tostig used cavalry to combat cross-border raids from Wales. Harold had also been in Normandy and seen William's cavalry in action.

26

to the NORTH...

EARLDOMS OF ENGLAND

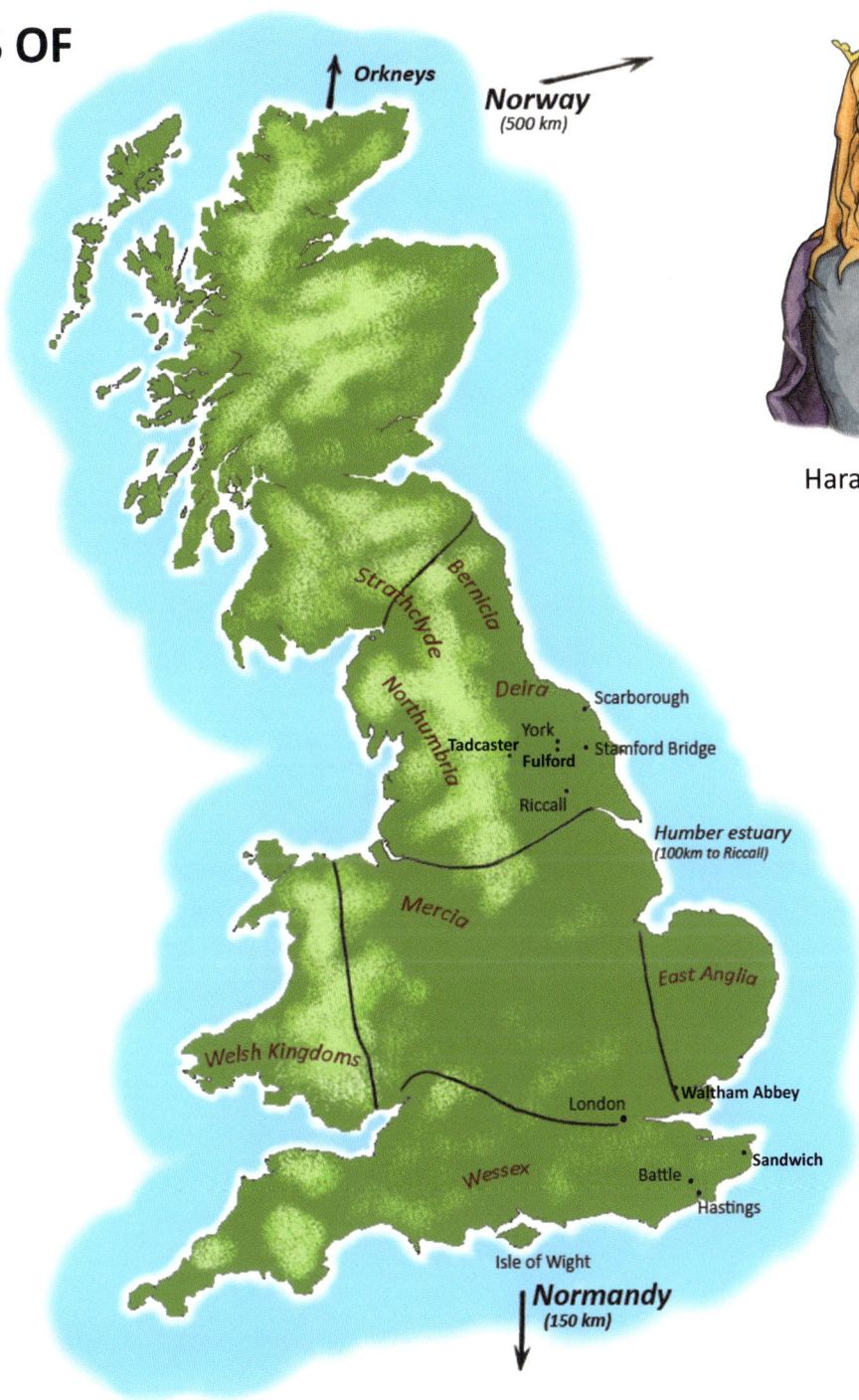

Orkneys

Norway
(500 km)

Harald 'Hardrada'

Strathclyde

Bernicia

Northumbria

Deira

Scarborough

Tadcaster • York • • Stamford Bridge
Fulford

Riccall

Humber estuary
(100km to Riccall)

Mercia

East Anglia

Welsh Kingdoms

Waltham Abbey

London •

Wessex

Battle • • Sandwich

Hastings

Isle of Wight

Normandy
(150 km)

William of Normandy

Harold reached Tadcaster and joined the Mercian army waiting there. But Earl Edwin, its leader, was probably still in York. Armies took orders only from their leader, so Edwin must have given permission for his army to obey Harold. Even though Harold was the king, the men from Mercia would not have known much about a king from far-away Wessex. This is where the marriage to Edwin's sister would have been so important, because Harold was now a part of the Mercian family.

Under the terms of surrender to King Harald of Norway, Earl Edwin could not have joined in the fighting: an oath was something sacred. When an Anglo-Saxon gave his oath it was trusted - this is what made stable government in England possible. Written charters were sometimes issued. These charters were signed by many witnesses whose job it was to see that the charter was respected. This was the beginning of the way we live today, with a set of written laws and people promising to uphold and enforce them.

How do we know this?
Most of our detailed knowledge about the people of this era comes from charters. These were normally grants of land or privilege. Charters are still being uncovered and translated and it should help historians to fill in gaps in our understanding of the times and the people.

England's King Harold could be just as cunning as King Harald of Norway. He made sure the Norsemen did not know the English army was coming. The battle had taken place at Fulford on Wednesday. On Sunday morning the people of York had submitted to the Norsemen.

But by Sunday evening, Harold had arrived and arranged for the gates of York to be closed and guarded, so news of his arrival did not leak out.

The Norsemen were expecting to exchange 300 hostages, so they did not take all their army to the agreed meeting place. Many of the Norse warriors were still resting or recovering after the battle at Fulford. The men did not even take their armour as they said it was too hot. Some probably left their shields behind to be repaired. So they were ill prepared for what happened next.

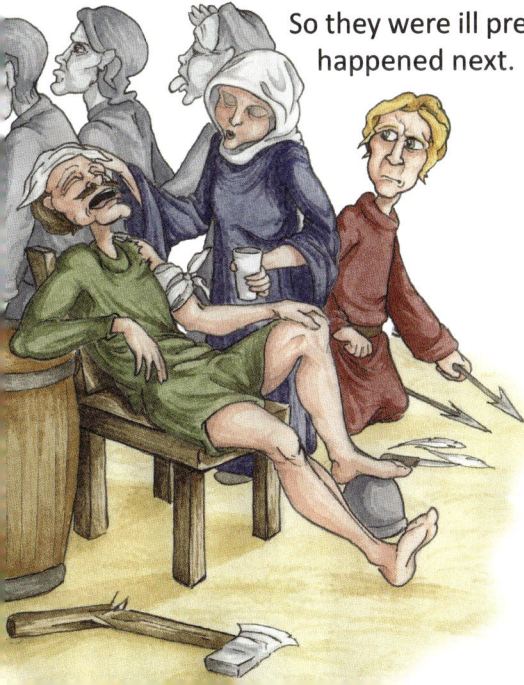

How do we know this?
We learn about Harold's plans from the chronicles. The exact timing comes from the Norse sagas but they might have been making excuses when they said the Norsemen did not take their armour. The sagas say they took many bows and arrows so perhaps they were hoping for some good hunting.

29

The landscape often plays an important part in battles. The land to the south and east of York was wetland. Harold and the English were able to advance along a moraine - a section of raised ground left by an ice age. The other King Harald followed another moraine further south with his Norsemen. It would be unlikely that either army would see the other as they marched. The wetland between them would stop scouts and messengers from discovering the other army. The two converged near a place we now call Stamford Bridge.

When the Norsemen crossed the River Derwent they left soldiers to guard each bridge and crossing place, which is what any good commander would do. They wanted to make sure the route back to their base at Riccall was protected. So the English were held up when they tried to cross.

A story is told of one axe-wielding warrior who was only removed when a spear was stuck up through the boards from below to dislodge him. The English were able to cross and stop the Norse army, with King Harald and Earl Tostig at its head, from returning to base. But the Norsemen did manage to get three galloping messengers back to Riccall to call for reinforcements.

How do we know this?

Historians do not normally study geology but in this situation it allows us to make sense of a strange situation - two armies marching towards each other without apparently knowing where the other was until it was too late. We cannot be certain about the story of the bridge, but similar stories appear throughout history and it makes military sense, just as it makes sense to attack the defender from below while others held his attention by attacking from the front. But the Norse sagas don't mention it and one chronicler says it happened during the retreat phase. It was later writers who suggested that it happened before the battle.

Both sides were now playing for time. The Norsemen were hoping for their reinforcements to arrive from Riccall. The English were waiting for their army to march from Tadcaster and cross the bridge - it takes several hours for a whole army to cross one bridge. Meanwhile, Harold used his new cavalry to harass the Norse army by charging at them. The Norsemen were trapped on a hillside with nothing to protect their flanks. This forced them to close ranks and form a circle or triangle using the limited number of shields on the outside. They stuck their spear shafts into the ground so the points created a barrier to stop the horses.

Before the battle began, Harold talked with his brother. Harold offered Tostig his title and position back in return for abandoning the Norse army. Tostig asked what terms were offered to King Harald of Norway. Harold joked that he could have only two metres of English soil, or perhaps a bit more because of his height. But Tostig had sworn an oath to serve the Norse king and he refused to join his brother. When ruthless King Harald 'Hardrada' heard about these negotiations he wanted to know why Tostig had not killed his brother!

How do we know this?
The geography allows us to make an informed guess about what happened. It would take time to get the message to Riccall, time for the army to get ready and many hours to rush along the rough tracks to get to the battle. Understanding this helps to explain the course of the battle and its outcome.

31

The fighting was fierce. The English would gallop up and throw their spears over the shields and in among the Norse army. King Harald of Norway grew tired of the cavalry attacks so he charged after the horsemen wielding his axe. He was hit in the throat by an arrow and killed.

With the Norse king dead, Harold stopped the battle to talk to his brother again. He repeated his offer but Tostig again refused. Tostig would not break his oath even though the man to whom he had given it was dead. The English soldiers then attacked while the cavalry chased the exhausted reinforcements that had run - in full armour - all the way from the Norse ships at Riccall to help their king. It was a hot day and the Norse sagas say that more died of heat exhaustion than at the hands of the English, or Saxons, as they call them.

Tostig was killed along with most of the Norse army near Stamford Bridge. In September it is dark by 8pm and a few warriors managed to escape from the battle. But it was about to get even worse for the Norsemen.

How do we know this?
Re-enactments allow us to see and test how ancient battles were fought. We know that a group of warriors who form a shield-wall can protect themselves. But isolated warriors cannot defend themselves if they are surrounded. So the brave but exhausted warriors arriving too late to save their king would have fallen quickly to Harold's mounted soldiers. We know this because 19 days later, the English army at Hastings would be victims of Norman horse troops in much the same way.

About the time the Norse warriors were racing from Riccall to save their king, the river tide turned. Now the Mercian fleet came down the river to attack those who had been left behind. The base was well protected from attack by the land: any attackers would have to cross long causeways and these would be easy to defend as they were just like a very long bridge - but without the possibility of being attacked from below. However, the base was vulnerable from attackers arriving by the river.

The Mercian seamen destroyed the Norse base. It is said the Norsemen needed only 30 ships to take the survivors bearing their sad news back to Norway. They left from somewhere near the modern city of Hull, perhaps using some of the supply vessels that had crossed with the longships, because their own ships must have been destroyed.

The sagas tell us that one of King Harald's daughters died of a broken heart at exactly the moment the battle raged. She had been going to marry King Harald's best war-leader, who led the Norsemen in their dash from Riccall, but he was killed. His brave mission is still remembered, and named in his honour, as Ore's Storm.

How do we know this?
The sagas and the Anglo-Saxon Chronicle give an outline of events but we need to study the landscape and tides to piece together how the Norse invasion was destroyed. We have to look at the various translations of the only chronicler to describe the chase to the ships and 'burning from behind'. The invaders had one victory at Fulford and were destroyed five days later. They had been in England for just one week.

33

Harold was still resting in York after his victory when news came a few days later that Duke William had landed in England. The Norman invasion fleet had sailed across at night, the ships following a lamp William put on the mast of his boat. William chose a quiet piece of the coast and landed at dawn so the English would not see the fleet coming.

Some ships got lost and were destroyed by defenders when they landed. But most of the army reached the long shingle beach at Pevensey, where it was practical to unload the men and horses. Over the next few days, William moved his army to Hastings where they would be much harder to attack.

The town of Hastings at that time was surrounded by wetland and there were only a few ways in. William had even brought a simple fort with him, called a bailey. These small wooden strong-points were often erected on a hill and would develop into stone forts, enabling the owner to dominate the people and land round about. From their secure base at Hastings, the invaders began to raid the surrounding countryside.

How do we know this?
Historians prefer written records but they have come to accept that the pictures in the Bayeux Tapestry also provide an informative record of some of the events surrounding the Norman invasion. We see the crossing by night and the construction of a fort at Hastings. The Tapestry was designed by monks at Canterbury and was embroidered by 'nuns' at various houses in the south of England. Many of what we call nuns were actually the widows of English warriors who were killed at Hastings. Convents and monasteries were an accepted place of refuge for such women.

Harold set off south again even though he was ill. When he reached London his brothers begged him to rest, saying they would fight Duke William because they had their armies ready for action. They thought Harold should wait for his own army, especially the cavalry, to re-assemble. Even the king's mother begged him not to go. He actually kicked her away - which, as it turned out, was foolish as well as rude.

Harold wanted to stop the raiding and probably thought he could block the few roads from Hastings. Once he had trapped the Norman invaders on the coast he would be able to wait a few days for reinforcements. His army and navy could then attack and destroy the Norman invasion.

But a good military plan needs to look at how the enemy might react. As it turned out, Harold had made a bad decision because William would not sit still and allow himself to be surrounded. While Harold and his brothers set out with an army from Kent and East Anglia hoping to trap William, the duke himself had other plans.

How do we know this?
An English monk called Orderic Vitalis gives us the details of the meeting with Harold's brothers. We are guessing at Harold's plan, but he was a clever commander and blockading William was a sensible idea. When writing history there are things that we know, others we can deduce with confidence and some where we just have to guess. So there are many occasions when we have to accept that a number of interpretations are possible.

Duke William was a good general. He had spent his whole life fighting. He knew the English were coming because his raiding parties and scouts would have told him. Instead of waiting around Hastings he took his troops out to meet the English. Perhaps he even hoped to get control of all the high ground before he was surrounded.

But King Harold reached the position first and the battle began the following morning. The Normans had their cavalry, which was a big advantage because the English cavalry had not arrived. Then again, the English occupied the high ground so the Norman cavalry had to charge up a steep hill. They could not break through the shield-wall. Horses have more sense than to charge a line of men with sharp spears pointing at them. This was just the noisy, first phase of a battle that would last all day. It also gave time for the foot troops and archers to get to the battle from their camps.

How do we know this?
Many French chroniclers recorded the battle. We think the early ones give an accurate report. We also know the landscape well as the site was turned into an abbey. It is possible to see what a good defensive position King Harold's army had.

William used his archers to harass the English shield-wall. This would damage shields and cause some injuries. After the archers, the cavalry returned. But the first turning point came when Harold's brothers led a charge to chase the cavalry, rather as King Harald of Norway had done so disastrously at Stamford Bridge. But not all the English shield-wall followed. Harold understood the danger posed by cavalry and wanted his troops to stay on the crest of the hill.

William used his cavalry to isolate the group that had charged and break it up so the warriors could be attacked from behind. Without their shield-wall and spears for protection the group was gradually cut down. Before long, two of Harold's brothers lay dead.

It was a long battle and both sides fought hard. They even stopped for lunch. But eventually a group of William's cavalry was able to break through and attack from behind, and this is when King Harold was killed. Since his brothers had already been slaughtered, the English army began to retreat. Duke William had won the battle.

How do we know this?
Again it is the French chroniclers who provide the best account of the battle. Their record makes sense from a military and landscape perspective. William showed great leadership and his army fought well. One other thing we know for certain is that Harold was not killed by an arrow in the eye. He became isolated and was cut down by mounted troops.

The battle took place on the south-facing slope of Senlac Hill, which was renamed Battle when William built an abbey and monastery there. But it would be confusing if it was called the battle of Battle, so we know this most famous clash as the battle of Hastings. All in all, within just 26 days in the year 1066 there were three major battles. And just as the English cavalry had done at Stamford Bridge, the Norman cavalry was able to win the day by chasing and destroying the retreating English.

Now William tried to go to London but his way was blocked. Young Edgar, the descendant of Alfred the Great, was proclaimed king, and the English prepared for a long war. William sent 200 knights to take London, but they met with resistance at Southwark and were driven off. The English now mustered another army, one with the rich city of London to support it. So William had another fight on his hands.

The situation was deadlocked: William could not capture London and the English would not surrender to an army no bigger than their own. So Duke William decided to play the politician rather than the warrior. The first important person to submit was Harold's sister, Queen Edith. Other cities were persuaded to open their gates to the Normans, but progress was slow.

How do we know this?
It is possible that we refer to 'the battle of Hastings' because Hastings is the place mentioned in the chronicles. There are detailed accounts in many of the chronicles about William's attempts to gain control of England. It is hard to understand why Queen Edith accepted William, since she had been the guardian of Edgar, who was now king of England. Edith's mother, Gytha, and other women from the Godwin family continued to resist the invaders until they were forced into exile in Flanders.

William spent three months negotiating with the English and made many promises to respect their old privileges. He needed English clerks and administrators in order to run such a prosperous country. And he needed to collect taxes to pay his army. The records kept by the English proved useful when William compiled the Doomsday Book 20 years later. This provided a central record of who owned what.

Only those who had been appointed by Harold were dismissed. Everybody else kept their job. The merchants of London were gradually won over with promises to respect their trading privileges. William's final victory did not come with a battle, but through negotiation.

On Christmas day 1066, the new abbey at Westminster witnessed the coronation of another king. The choice of Christmas day for the ceremony was part of William's plan to demonstrate that he had a divine right to the throne of England. He had told his followers that they were fighting to defend the true religious faith in England.

But the day was not a success. The Archbishop of Canterbury refused to perform the ceremony. At one point the soldiers protecting William mistook cheering from the spectators for a popular uprising and attacked everyone outside, setting fire to surrounding houses. These attacks only stopped when William appeared at the abbey door.

How do we know this?
The English and French chronicles report these events and tell us William 'took great pains to please everybody'. The Doomsday Book remains an invaluable source of information. There are many references to the value and size of holdings before the conquest so we know that the record-keeping established by King Alfred was still operating.

Norman lords did not live in a hall among their people, but in castles. This was one of the key changes in England after 1066. First, motte and bailey strongholds were erected around the country. Later, these were replaced by stone-built towers and forts where the new lords of the English would be safe from surprise attack. William lived outside London at Barking until a fort was built to protect him. Then he moved into what we still know as the Tower of London.

It was to Barking that the earls Edwin and Morcar came in January 1067 to accept William as their king. Within a year they would recognise that this had been a mistake, and would go on to lead revolts that would occupy William for the rest of his life. It did them no good: Edwin was eventually murdered and Morcar died in a dungeon.

We don't know what happened to their sister, Harold's wife Ealdgyth, but we think that she gave birth to twins in Chester and the family probably fled to Ireland when her brothers submitted to William.

How do we know this?
We are lucky to have many sources describing what happened. They tell us that key people were quickly brought over from Normandy and given important jobs in the church and monasteries. We also hear that Edwin and Morcar joined William when he went back to Normandy. There was even talk of a marriage to one of his daughters. But it appears they soon understood that the Norman way of ruling was very different to the one they were used to.

By 1069 the rebellions had begun, and King Sweyn arrived with an army from Denmark. King William offered him Danegeld to stop Sweyn joining the rebels who were fighting in the Fens of East Anglia and in the north of England. King William was under attack from all sides: Harold's sons were attacking the West Country; Edgar with the Scots and Northumbrians was capturing everything north of York; and the Welsh attacked Shrewsbury and Chester. Forests had become unsafe for Norman soldiers; many stories of 'green-wood men', such as Robin Hood, survive to this day.

King William responded to the uprisings with a fast-moving campaign, followed by the destruction of everything in the northern rebel lands. This is known as 'the harrowing of the north'. England had lost many leaders in 1066 and young Edgar did not have an army, so there was nobody to unite the country. The English had no answer to the castles that allowed the new rulers to dominate the towns and countryside. And King William was a very good general.

In 1070, Pope Gregory VII issued a tariff of penances for those who had taken part in Duke William's invasion of England. The invaders had claimed to be on a crusade to impose Christian rule against an enemy of the Church of Rome. This was how they won the Pope's support for the invasion in the first place, but it turned out that it was not really true.

How do we know this?
The chroniclers outline the events of the rebellions, and it is the Doomsday Book that shows just how badly the north was devastated. Estates that had supported many families before are listed as abandoned.

41

The Norman rulers brought many changes to the English way of life. Perhaps the most important was that the people now owed duties to their overlord and had very few rights. Before the conquest people had to serve their overlord, but in exchange their lord was responsible for their security and welfare. The ancient word for lord meant 'loaf-giver'. Under the new, feudal system that evolved in England after the Norman conquest the overlord had all the rights, while the responsibilities to do all the work rested with the ordinary people.

But there were some brighter spots. We have almost no record of Norman women moving to England, so Norman men probably married local women and their children grew up speaking English. It is interesting that we find Norman words used for the food that only the rich could afford, but we keep the English word for the animal themselves.

We tend to remember the Magna Carta, which was signed in 1215, as restoring some of the rights that the people of England had enjoyed. But as early as 1100, King William's youngest son, King Henry I, had introduced a Charter of Liberties which did something to recognise the rights of the population.

How much do we really know?
There are many ways to tell our story. If you read today's newspapers each one will offer a slightly different version of yesterday's events. You need to tease out the truth from all the different accounts because not everybody sees the same events in the same way. This detective work is what makes the study of the past such fun. Fresh clues are being uncovered by researchers, archaeologists and other scholars. So it is important that we go back and look at the evidence again. There are always lessons to be learnt.

Most people think that studying the past helps us understand why things happened the way they did. If we understand why some things went wrong and others worked out well, we might be able to make better decisions in the future. But we also have to accept that we need to live with different versions of our story, and realise that debate and disagreement are a part of the process.

GLOSSARY

Abduct – To take away by force and without permission; it has the same meaning as the word kidnap.

Ambassador – Someone who acts a messenger or representative for somebody but often for a country and its rulers.

Besiege – To surround a place with your army so the people inside are trapped.

Chronicle – A written record of historical events which is set down by the chronicler without much interpretation or comment.

Consecration – Normally a religious ceremony when something or someone is committed to serve that religion.

Converge – To move together until they meet.

Expeditionary force – A travelling army which would go where it was sent, rather than one only prepared to defend its local area. The British armies in both the first and Second World Wars were both called BEFs, or British Expeditionary Forces.

Exile – Being forced to live away from your home or country.

Flank – The edges of an army. No commander wants their enemy to sneak round the edges and attack it from behind.

Kin – A word that covers all one's relatives and family.

Lure – Tempt or attract somebody to do something, often as part of a trick.

Penance – An action that is done to show that you are sorry - like an apology, only you actually have to do something to say sorry.

Political – Dealing with the affairs of government or involving the behaviour of leaders. But political also means that the actions are designed to serve the objectives of a person.

Refuge – A place of safety.

Retreat – The word that armies like to use when they decide to run away.

Saga – A historical or mythical story that was used in Norse lands to record events. They are often in the form of poetry to help people remember them, until writing became common in the 13th Century when they were written down.

Speculate – Often used instead of the word 'think' when all the evidence is not available.

Traitor – Somebody you trust and who changes sides to fight against you.

Viking and Norse – The two words both describe the Scandinavian peoples (from Norway, Denmark and Sweden) who traded and raided widely. Their raids in the eighth to the tenth centuries gave them a fearsome reputation. Norse just means 'from the north' but the origin of the word Viking is uncertain.

MORE READING

Lost days (page 17): http://en.wikipedia.org/wiki/Gregorian_calendar.
The Gregorian calendar was adopted in Britain in 1752, rather later than most. It was necessary to remove 11 days so Wednesday, 2 September 1752 was followed by Thursday, 14 September in 1752.

Lady Godiva (page 19): http://en.wikipedia.org/wiki/Lady_Godiva
Her name occurs in charters and the Domesday book. The Old English name Godgifu or Godgyfu meant "gift of God". Godiva was the Latin version.

Fulford - read more about the site and present day investigations into the battle at www.fulfordbattle.com

Anglo Saxon Chronicles: http://en.wikipedia.org/wiki/Anglo_Saxon_Chronicles
Or read them for yourself: http://www.gutenberg.org/etext/657

The Chronicle of the kings of Norway, as assembled by Snorri Sturlson.
Also known as the *Heimskringla*:
http://www.gutenberg.org/etext/598

Doomsday Book (page 39): http://en.wikipedia.org/wiki/Domesday_Book

ABOUT THE CREATORS

Charles Jones is the author of a number of history books including *The Forgotten Battle of 1066 – Fulford* (History Press, 2007). Find out more at www.ourcreativecommunity.org.

Amanda Pollard works as a freelance illustrator. Previous projects have included educational posters, illustrations for the national press and a variety of private commissions. Take a closer look at www.illustratedbyamanda.co.uk.

Printed in the United States
1457LVUK00002B